The Five BLAC Heartbeats

Of

Love and Wealth

Queen Tiffany Geselle and King Donte'

As you journey through this book remember this

Love is progression. A partnership between two unique people who bring out the very best in each other. They know that even though they are wonderful as individuals they are even better as a team.

---- BLAC Heartbeat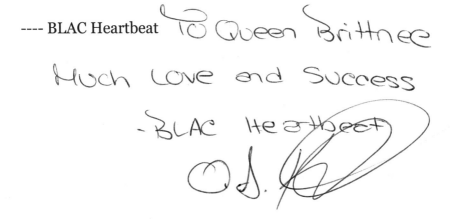

To Queen Brittnee

Much Love and Success

-BLAC Heartbeat

O.J.

We dedicate this book to our son King Jayden. Every sacrifice and investment we make, every challenge we have to face and every obstacle we have to overcome is for the purpose of giving you a better life full of experiences and opportunities. Our sole purpose is to show you how to be the best version of yourself by being the best version of ourselves.

We Love You!

Contents

● ●

•••

Do You Still Believe in Love?

We want you to know that true love and healthy relationships still exist. Never sell yourself short from what you deserve and always remember, you have the power in you to make the changes you need to make and to receive the things you want to receive if you want those things bad enough.

Everyone always asks us how we do it. How did we get "lucky" enough to find the person that fit our puzzle? How did we leave the corporate 9-5 and start 3 successful businesses? How did we start a family that is strong and rock-solid even though we've never seen what that looks like growing up. Why did we create BLAC Heartbeat?

Queen Tiffany Geselle

I was born and raised in Lefrak City, Queens, NY and spent most of my youth in Southside Jamaica, Queens and the Westside of Harlem. I grew up around dope dealing, homicides, teen pregnancy domestic abuse and like most kids where I come from I never witnessed any positive black relationships. My father was one of the biggest drug dealers in N.Y. in the 80's and ended up having 9 kids and served a 13 ½ year prison sentence when I was 7 years old. Despite the circumstances, my mother did her best in making sure I had everything I needed and didn't get caught up in the lifestyle around us.

Unfortunately there wasn't a guaranteed way for me to escape the lifestyle everyone was living. From young I was all about getting money. Around 15 my father and I started communicating through letters from prison and the shift in my mindset started to happen. He was giving me game about life, boys/men, sex, being a woman, business and ownership from behind prison walls. Things that only a man could teach a girl at such a risky age. Risky because it was too easy to get caught up around that time.

Although my father was absent he came at a critical point in my life. By 20 years old I was tired of the cycle and I knew I wanted more for myself. I knew that in order for me to have an opportunity to be successful in life and relationships I needed to leave my environment. So I woke up one Tuesday morning and decided it was time. I took all the money I had and bought a flight to Atlanta, GA. With $20, 2 suitcases and no plan, I knew if I left there was no turning back. I was on a mission to create the life I wanted. That's where my journey of getting to know myself began.

Like so many young black women and men I was the product of a broken family. But that did not define who I had the potential to be and what I believed I deserved for my life. Don't let your past determine your future. People may not understand your growth or potential but everyone will appreciate your choices in due time.

King Donte

I'm from the Northside of Toledo, OH. Rockingham to be exact. If you know anything about Toledo, you know that it's considered the Mud for a reason. In the late 80's and early 90's, drugs, pimping, hoeing, and gang affiliation was the environment I was exposed to growing up. I was the oldest of my siblings in a city that raised hustlers, and it forced me to grow up faster than any kid would want to.

Along with the hustle, I naturally adopted some of the cheating, lying and selfish behavior that I saw around me my entire life. **Be careful of learned behavior**. I made decisions that contributed to the downfall of some relationships, yet I always knew I had the potential to be a good man for the right woman. So when it was time to take a real hard honest look at myself, who I was and what I was doing, I had to face my own reality, I was becoming the kind of man I spent my life looking down on. The men who hurt my mother and sisters.

I wanted a wife and family at some point in my life and I knew I needed to be my best self for them, so I decided to do some self-work. I fasted from dating and sex for a while. I cut off negative people and started learning about myself and what it meant to be a God. I started to pay attention to what I needed instead of simply what I wanted.

The Hustler Meets the Goddess

So how did we end up authors, successful business owners and in a marriage that thrives off being with your best friend every day? It's simple, with the will and drive to put ourselves in a better situation, we realized we could achieve everything we desired if we believed in ourselves, believed in each other and put in the work. Meaning, we both had to leave our environments in search of something different, something better. We didn't want to be those people who settled for living an unhappy and unfulfilled life. We had to get rid of the learned behavior that caused us to be in non-productive relationships and learn how to grow into the people were meant to be. It took time energy and patience but we did it, and by the time we met, we were in a position to understand each-others background but appreciate each-others will and effort to want and do better. It was a bold move on both ends to believe that we deserved more than what we saw growing up and actually make the changes necessary to get it.

We want our experiences and the success of our relationship to be an example to those who may have given up on the idea of love or those who have settled.

Everything in this book is based on real life experiences from ourselves and other BLAC Heartbeats around the country. The lessons we have learned throughout the years on how to build a solid union and gain wealth with your partner is knowledge that can change the game for people who come from similar backgrounds. Here's the beauty of relationships, not every relationship is the same or follow the same rules. Only you and your partner can determine what wealth means to you individually and as a team.

We wrote this book because we want to pass this knowledge on to as many people as we can. To enjoy the benefits of having a teammate who helps you build in every area of your life. When we begin to go back to loving ourselves, our families and our community then and only then will we begin to build wealth and ownership on a grand scale.

We choose to inspire and motivate men and women to take a look at themselves and their relationships to see how they can grow and change the cycle of dysfunctional relationships they may be used to. You owe it to yourselves to consider some new methods and apply proven strategies to improve upon your current dating or relationship experience. **This book is an investment in your future.**

••

Overcoming the Lows in Relationships

Since we have been together we've been calling each other soulmates. This was after all the ups and downs of our past relationships and learning that love shouldn't hurt, drain you or weaken your growth. We always say that life is our biggest teacher and at some point we have to take responsibility for who we choose to be and who we choose to be with. We were watching a video online and a young lady in her early twenties was sitting in her car. She was brown skin, slim and very animated as she expressed her views on women who don't please their men. The young lady gave a deep description of all the lows men go through when their significant other isn't pleasing them. In her words she stated, "How do these women have these good guys and still screw them over." She expressed over and over again how other women complain about their man even though he takes care of home. She then makes a bold statement saying women like herself love swooping in and taking these good guys from their women and treating them as Kings.

We wonder why after coaching so many couples we find that the number one issue in the black community is infidelity. As we discuss in the section "Family is Wealth" the odds are stacked against black people because of incarceration, racial profiling, government assistance, and lack of knowledge to assist in financial freedom. "Good" black men are a hot commodity. Reason being, so many men are locked up or can't get a job due to having a record. This results in them engaging in criminal activities to try to provide for themselves and their families. This creates a shortage of good black men causing some women to settle for any man just to not be alone or to say they have someone. What kind of relationship is that?!

Relationships are an investment, so to be with someone "just because" is not enough. Marriage is supposed to be a bonus, as this is and will always be a business decision. The love and affection for one another should never die. This is the glue that sustains the energy to build your future together. The Five BLAC Heartbeats prove that if you are truly meant to be together, when faced with life's obstacles, you both will have the faith in each other to know as a union you will continue progressing.

Our greatest sacrifice is allowing ourselves to die daily. This just means out with the old and in with the new. Marriage says you're ready to let go of childish ways and begin investing in one another. Question, why even take the leap if so many people are going to continue living like they are single? Studies show that pressure, religion, arrangements, green cards, pregnancy and money were at top of the list. In these cases, no one really has a true purpose for progression and building with each other, there is no spark after the honey moon phase because there was no substance to begin with.

For our couples looking at taking the leap of faith and combine kindred spirits, remember to set goals that determine what you both want for your futures. This ensures you and your partner are on the same page with where you see your lives going. See marriage as a business decision, the investment of a lifetime. My wife and I flirted with the decision in our past relationships, and she can attest to the fact that I took it very serious when committing all the way. Divorce was not an option, as we didn't want to give that type of negative energy to our union resulting in departure. Too many times we hear how our people place separation plans in their arsenal. This brings about that energy and manifests the troubles that will soon follow because you have already convinced yourselves that it won't last. So stop planning for the worst. Instead, counter that negative mindset and set goals leading to progressive thoughts and sexual transmutation. We all face lows in relationships married or not. The key to union is actually taking yourself out of the equation, and understanding your partner from the beginning. So for our long term and married couples that may find themselves in trying times, look closely at your investment (partner) and ask yourself these questions. Can this love I have levitate every aspect of my dreams? If your partner has changed over time, ask yourself, Can I live with my partner's new attitude and is my outlook about life aligned with theirs? Do I need to grow to meet them where they are? Or do they need to grow to meet me where I am?

Power Moves for Power Couples

When people mention power couples people usually talk about the likes of Jay Z and Beyoncé or Will Smith and

Jada Pinkett Smith. But don't think that because you are not in a Jay-Z and Beyoncé tax bracket that you cannot create a power couple dynamic within your own relationship. And don't for a second think that because they are considered power couples they don't come across issues in their relationships. To us, a power couple is one that is continually progressing. Setting goals together for the benefit of their future. They find ways to enjoy life while knocking out the goals. Resulting in the life they both dream of. Here are some tips on how to create a power couple flow in your relationship.

Paid-cations. Idle time is the devil's workshop. We all know todays couples are highly influenced by the superficial world controlled by reality TV and social media. Instead of wasting time watching others put on ratchet entertainment, take your relationship to the next level and have fun doing it. Escaping from the day to day motion picture of the four walls we live in is something we all need from time to time. When we talk about vacations for our couples, we suggest cruises, retreats and trips out of the country. What if you both created Paid-cations? As partners we promote goal setting and we are always finding ways to spread our movement. What is a Paidcation? Paid-cations are simply vacations that serve the purpose of making money while you're enjoying time away from home. Together you can see the world while letting your coins stack. The road life makes your creative juices flow and with both of you having goals, chasing them will give life to your relationship and give you the opportunity to see your partner in a different light.

Sex Sex and more Sex. We will elaborate more on this subject in our "Let's Talk About Sex" section. We want our readers to know how important sex is for the success of a power couple. Create sexy mind blowing intimacy while transmuting your wealth seeking thoughts. Make sure both of you have the same intention and agree on the thoughts you want to manifest. This is so important and we can't say it enough, sex is good, but sex is power if shared with the right person. Put your partner's needs ahead of yours when focusing on how to please them. You will both reach highs that naturally transition into wealth building.

Satisfy your Temple. See your partner as your temple. The same way you take care of your temple (body), take care of your spouse with the same commitment. If more couples took the time out to worship one another, they would definitely recognize the power in union. We're talking about motivating each other mentally, body sculpting (working out together), praying and meditating together. Designate one day every week that is strictly dedicated to you and your partner. We call our day BLAC Friday and every Friday we create an experience that we both will remember and enjoy. This may be a picnic in the house in the middle of the floor, a trip to the top of a parking deck watching the stars with the sun roof open, instead of watching a movie we might create a movie (sex scene) all in good fun, or play chess to expand our strategy skills. We do these activities to show each other how much we appreciate having been given the opportunity to share air with one another and take advantage of the moments spent together.

We want you to benefit from what the Five BLAC Heartbeats will do for you and your relationship. These five keys are necessary for the investment in one another to pay off and a guide on how to transition from an average couple to a power couple.

· ·

Family is Wealth

In a country full of diversity among cultures, religions and nationalities, it's not surprising why we still experience racism today. The U.S. is a melting pot of various races who each bring their own identity based on ancestral and spiritual understanding. All races except African Americans have an understanding about their native land and beliefs. As black people we were stripped of our native tongue, heritage and true spiritual/religious practices so long ago that it seems to have never existed. Slavery with the help of the Willie Lynch speech was an agenda to force us to fight against each other and devalue family and community. In 1712 the Willie Lynch documents said their plan would keep blacks enslaved for over 300 years. And even today, blacks still suffer from the mentality forced upon us by our ancestor's oppressors. This is why today you see black men being hunted and shot down in the street like wild animals (they have more sympathy over the killing of animals than they do the murders of our black men).

We want to assist in the empowerment of restructuring the black family. The effects of ending slavery proved that most black people had no idea how to live without depending on the very people who enslaved us. Black people had little to no ownership in land or property. Jails were built in high numbers to keep black men confined (another form of slavery). The prison system dismantled black families making sure black males weren't present in the household and forcing the mothers to take on the role of the absent father (one of the reasons society deems black women angry today).

But with practice, truth and strategies we can get back our mental and economic strength and truly manifest the lives we want to live. To our black men, don't get discouraged by circumstances or financial setbacks. If you have children, even if you have multiple kids with different women, see the blessing in your family and use it to your advantage. Teach your kids the business by hiring them first. This keeps the money in house while empowering your children to embrace ownership. If we begin to use some proven business practices in structuring our families and communities we will elevate our race, empower our children, create employment opportunities, rebuild families and build wealth. If we take the same dedication we have for tithing in churches and commit to building long term wealth through a community sou-sou, as a family and community we could all be in positions to buy land, property and start businesses using cash. This would cut down mortgages drastically, secure land, eliminate interest rate based business loans, and create an opportunity to rewrite history.

Family is wealth and with the right understanding you will find that family is the key to truly being successful. We call it ALL HANDS ON DECK and everyone needs to play a role. We are all born as Kings and Queens and we are here to bless this planet with our GOD given talent.

Why aren't more black families owning retail stores, grocery stores, fitness centers, banks and real estate? If more black people came together to create sou-sou's we would be so far removed from poverty in a short matter of time. We keep mentioning this word sou-sou and we're sure you're wondering what this is. A **sou-sou** is a Nigerian term and it's a savings arrangement where a group of people each pool an equal amount of money for a period of time (month, two weeks, etc) and after that time is up, one person in the group gets all that money. They keep doing this till everyone gets their turn and receives that full lump sum at least once. Instead of getting a loan through a bank and paying interest rates you can get a few trust worthy people to create and invest in a community sou-sou. This concept will immediately put black people in power and on a path to community wealth. The power is in numbers!

Breaking the Cycle

When we build strong healthy relationships throughout the entire spectrum of our community, family, friends, romantic, and entrepreneurial, we show the world we are more than criminals and bitter black women. The world is afraid of the power of strong black families because in numbers we can regain power of our own government and economy.

Ladies, start by taking more time to find the Goddess in yourselves. We are the essence of every living breathing thing created. Understand your worth and embrace your beauty. Speak to you womb. Forgive yourselves. Forgive others that hurt you. Many of us suffer from the fatherless syndrome. Once we heal from our trauma we can become the Queens we are.

Recognize and appreciate the goddess in other women. Support each other, invest in and with each other, encourage each other and stop the jealous behavior and competing with one another. Black women are the most unappreciated and disrespected people in this country and it primarily comes from other black women and black men. It has to stop! The world is already against us, so we have to be the ones to band together to encourage change. You have to realize how much of a force you are when you stick together than if you are separated and fighting against one another. Queens, we have to respect each other if we expect the men to respect and protect us.

Treat your man as the King he is (once he proves worthy) and show him that in a world full of hate and fear, he is loved. Remind him that he is needed and that you're here to support him. You are his queen, be his peace and his refuge. Stop letting your past or society tell you that you shouldn't submit to your man. Understand that you can be independent and submissive at the same time. Submissive simply means taking care of his needs and he should be taking care of yours just the same. Stop nagging over nothing, control your attitudes and emotions and stop making it more difficult than it has to be. It may sound harsh but it's reality. Most of the men we've come across told us that their main issue is being with someone who doesn't appreciate them and what they do. Constantly arguing with them about things that aren't important instead of together creating a situation that encourages partnership. Get back to what's important. Being in love, being happy, family, good health, spirituality and financial freedom. If it doesn't have anything to do with you being happy, leave it alone.

Men, take the time to find out who you are instead of what everyone wants or expects you to be. Think about the people who depend on you. Recognize that if you brought children into this world, you are responsible for their wellbeing despite the circumstances. In all of your relationships, be there, be present. Build with other men and invest in one another. Don't be discouraged by your environment, circumstances or relationships. Use those challenges as fuel to make sure your kids and family won't have to face the same stumbling block you did. So many men use the excuse of them not having a role model or father figure to teach them how to be a man as a way to get out of being responsible. At some point you have to let that go and choose who and what you want to be in this life and fight for it.

Respect your queen. You should take pride in your woman. Always push her to be her best while encouraging her to follow her dreams and live a full life. If you have a good woman place her on a throne and let her know she can never be replaced. Appreciate her for all that she is, acknowledge her strengths constantly and massage her insecurities so you can break down her walls of self-doubt and past pain. Recognize her power, she can be the answer to all of your questions about life. Be her strength when needed and show her that her imperfections make her perfect. Get in tune with her spirit.

Read this book with an open mind and open heart. Our goal is to remove the patterns of learned behavior that have been holding us back from reaching our true potential. Be open to the change and we guarantee you will see growth in your life and how you approach relationships.

....

The Five BLAC Heartbeats of Love and Wealth

"They Don't Believe in Love So Why Would They Believe in Us"- Floacist

The Five BLAC Heartbeats of Love and Wealth are not only guiding principles for building a loving committed relationship. They are also character enhancers and developers that will really help you create a solid foundation on your road to securing financial freedom with your partner and for your family. Recognizing equal partnership in love and business is the purpose of this book.

The five building blocks we (will) focus on are Friendship and Courting, Consideration, Appreciation, Trust and Security.

When you look at these concepts from a business perspective you will find a direct correlation between love and business. We will show you how to use these (tools) building blocks to enhance your current and future relationships.

Any information in this book is not considered legal advice. Please consult a legal or financial advisor for any legal advice.

Let's build wealth!!!

••

FRIENDSHIP & COURTING

BLAC HEARTBEAT #1

1. **Friend**- *A relationship of mutual affection between people.*

"Build a friendship before a relationship, then watch your empire grow"—BLAC Heartbeat

Friendship is the first fundamental lesson of the Five BLAC Heartbeats of Love and Wealth. Everything that comes after is nonexistent if friendship is not built first. Why spend precious time with someone you can't grow with and get money with at the same time. Wealth is not always a monetary gain, but any type of mutual gain for the benefit of your future. People have to stop looking at the satisfaction of the moment, and think about the long term value someone can bring into their life.

The word friendship should not be used lightly once you begin to understand its power. In love and in business, you should be in a partnership with someone who you can trust as a friend, someone who is dependable and responsible. So when taking friendship into consideration, shouldn't it be the goal in any relationship, to be in love with your best friend? If so, what it takes to build a friendship with your partner is not a difficult process at all. Building friendship with a potential partner starts with the art of courting. Courting is taking the time to get to know your partner before dedicating yourself to him/her but we'll get to that later.

Defining Friendship

Integrity, honesty and dependability are some of the core traits you should look for when considering building friendship with a potential partner. This person should be on a similar mental wave length as you based on where you are in life. When a person has these kinds of values they are more likely to have your best interests at heart once you become partners.

There are so many benefits to being friends before you start dating someone and definitely before you decide to commit. We see a lot of relationships fail and are short lived because people rush into them, not truly knowing the person they are investing their time in. Physical attraction is usually the reason why people jump into relationships, but looks fade especially when their personal appearance is attractive but their attitude and personality is foul. It's better to have a foundation that is built on trust and understanding rather than basing it solely on physical or sexual attraction. There is nothing wrong with taking time to connect on a friendship level before diving into a relationship. It shows how genuine both people are in potentially wanting something more.

Often people jump into what they think is a relationship but really it's just a sexual escapade. Ladies, have you ever felt like if you didn't have sex with your partner or someone you were dealing with, they would go find pleasure elsewhere or not want to be with you at all? Guys have you ever been in a situation with a woman you were into but when you had sex things started to change?

One of you became more attached and emotional while the other was fine with the way things were. These realities only come about because there is no true friendship that exists between you and it creates an emotional imbalance. Sex is an expression of intimacy and should be of mutual benefit to all parties involved. When it's done with people who have developed a friendship first and moved into a relationship or union second, the sex becomes a way to touch the spirit of a person. Although sex is vital in a relationship it can't be the only reason you are with someone. Sex can be a distraction and it can confuse you from knowing who a person really is if it's the only thing you both have in common.

You deserve to take the time to make sure a person is worthy of you in your most precious state. People should look for someone who can satisfy them inside and outside the sheets. So if you are entertaining friends with benefits, take it for what it is and don't expect it to be anything more than that.

We took 5 people who were dating and in new relationships and challenged them to ask their partner or potential partner these questions while we coached them along their journey. What do I gain or benefit from you and what do you gain or benefit from me? This allowed them to lay everything out on the table to limit any confusion about each persons expectations in a relationship. It allowed them to build a friendship off communication and honesty without being judged or having so many emotions attached early on. It opened them up to get to know each other's pet peeves and habits that may have been deal breakers had they not been friends first.

If you are dating or in a relationship that is not providing what you need, we suggest you ask these questions. How can we be of benefit to each other? It forces both people to think about what they bring to the table and what they need their partner to bring to the table. It brings about an open honest conversation about goals and expectations. If they can't, don't want to, or are afraid to answer those questions, you should seriously consider reevaluating that friendship/relationship ASAP. Don't be afraid to let people go if their definition of friendship is not the same as yours. Better to know sooner than later to avoid disappointment because one of you is not satisfied. Friends hold each other accountable for what they say they are going to do. So why should this be any different with your partner?

"It's not a lack of love, but a lack of friendship that makes unhappy relationships" – Friedrich Nietzsche

Relationships and Wealth

My wife and I understood from the beginning friendship had to be the basis of our relationship if we were going to pursue love and wealth together in the future. Consistency, respect and communication were some of the pillars that contributed in us intersecting relationship, love and business.

Too many times people get romantically involved with each other way before they learn who the other person is, only to realize later they're not in a relationship, they're in a "situationship". Relationships should be easy when you're in love with your best friend. Your soulmate should be a reflection of you. I get compliments daily from other men and women about how amazing my wife is and it makes me proud because as a union she is a reflection of me.

Sometimes men and women fail to see their partner for who they really are. They want their partner to be who they expect them to be and they go into a relationship trying to change the person. No one should be in a relationship where they are not accepted for being themselves. When you develop a friendship first you learn the true character of a person. Relationships blossom when two individuals come together as a union without losing their individuality.

We need to not lose focus of our intent when it comes to meeting or being with that perfect person. Can you be totally honest about what it is that you want from your better half? Can you see that person delivering on what they say can benefit you? These are some questions to ask yourself about the character of your partner.

Like it is with business partners (friends), your soulmate needs to be someone you can invest in and build with. If you're currently in a relationship, evaluate where you are at this point. What goals have you both set? Goal setting keeps you both honest even if it's something as light as each of you putting away $100 a month for a vacation later in the year.

This investment brings forth such good energy that guarantees some type of growth within your relationship. You talk about the trip, you envision it, you get excited about putting the money away, and together you count down the days until your getaway. It gives you both something to look forward to and keeps the positive energy flowing throughout your relationship. You'll always have a positive conversation piece that can overshadow any negative situation that might occur. It shows how serious your partner is about your future together. More importantly, it creates an understanding about working together as a team. Once you accomplish this one goal, you are more likely to keep challenging yourselves to create new goals, and plans to achieve them.

Some couples may look at their relationship as being a way to past time or fill a void. Relationships like this do not produce the substance needed to grow.

Staying in a relationship just because you've been with this person for a long time, because you have children together, or because you have emotional ties is called settling. What if we told you that having assets and investments as it pertains to business can help build and restructure the values within your union? Yes, relationships are businesses decisions, and people should have some type of awareness of this, being that the number 1 reason for divorce in America is finances. If we can show you how starting a business with your partner will free up time and build a legacy for your family and for your loved ones would you consider making a few changes in your relationship?

Evaluate your Friendship with your Partner or People you are Dating

Think about the person you are with or considering making a partner and answer the questions below.

What types of conversations are you having daily?

Are those conversations encouraging and supportive?

Does he/she hold you accountable for your actions in a positive way?

Is he/she stagnant and not going anywhere in life or is he/she goal oriented and taking action?

What strengths do you bring to a relationship?

What strengths does he/she bring into a relationship?

How can you both bring your strengths together to meet a common goal or build a future together?

If you find that you and your partner need to get back to rebuilding a friendship start with simply having fun. Having fun will open people up to feel comfortable about having conversations. Here's some suggestions

- Get a bottle of wine, put some music on, dance and play cards
- Go out to watch a football or basketball game
- Workout together; gym, bike riding, race at the park
- Order take out, talk about some books (The Five BLAC Heartbeats of Love and Wealth)—ask them what they think about the topics in this book and have a discussion about them.

••

FRIENDSHIP & COURTING

CONTINUATION.....

1. **Courting-** *the activities that occur when people are developing a romantic relationship that could lead to marriage or the period of time when such activities occur*

"Dating is usually about meeting a selfish need. Courting is about intentionally building a foundation for a long term commitment or marriage."-BLAC Heartbeat

In a society that's all about getting quick results, we lost focus of what it takes to start and maintain a strong foundation in relationships. Courting is what builds the substance that relationships thrive off of. It takes time and consistency and it allows people to become friends first, learn each other's likes and dislikes, digs into a person's true character and explore someone's goals and dreams. It really allows you to see the God in a person.

When we got together we courted from day 1 and it hasn't stopped yet. Courting has been an important part of the success of our relationship because we took the time to find out each other's likes and dislikes. We spent time talking about what books we read and the things we've learned from our experiences in life. We learned each other's core values and what we wanted for our future. We asked the important questions about how we viewed marriage and children. What we thought about intimacy and spirituality.

The things we learned we had in common were being affectionate, being honest, sexual exploration, and the desire to own property one day. We both had a passion and plans to own our own thriving business that would allow us to quit our 9-5. Then we broke some of those things we have in common down even further.

When it came to affection we talked about the benefits of being affectionate in a relationship as a giver or receiver of affection. We talked about how some people find it hard to be affectionate and how that can be a drag on a relationship.

As a woman I was able to tell my future husband what affection meant to me.... Spending time together, small things like kissing, being engaged when we are having conversations and effortless physical interaction.

As a man I was able to tell my future wife what affection meant to me.... Quality time, physical touch and positive words of affirmation speaking to my spirit, teaching me and encouraging me.

We were able to explore how affection or the lack thereof impacted some of the relationships we witnessed growing up and with that understanding we talked about how important it is to stay in tune with your partners needs in the area of affection.

For business, we talked about my husband's strengths being sales and management while my strengths were contracts, administration, finances and keeping the business afloat from behind the scenes. He was more of the sales person and I liked the backend work. Once we identified each other's strengths and how we could put them to use to build wealth in all areas of our life, we knew that it was more than a physical attraction and we had the potential to be a great team.

People these days are afraid to be honest and have important conversations early on. Most people put up a front to show their best selves, but are not honest about the areas that need work. Many women are not open about their views on dating and sex and most men are not open about what they want for their future. Some women feel as though if they tell a man they don't want to have sex until marriage that it will run the man off. While some women refrain from being honest about their sexual appetite in fear that a man will only want a sexual relationship. Some men think if they tell a woman about where they are in life or where they want to be, the woman will attempt to use them for what they have or judge them for what they do not.

We have found that one of the biggest mistakes women make in relationships is not asking for what they truly want. They are not honest about what they want and need in a relationship causing them to be dissatisfied or disappointed down the line. Instead they settle for what's available or only ask for what they think they can have. Men are simple creatures and would rather clearly be told what a woman wants so they can provide it. Not being honest and clear about your expectations and desires will eventually lead to bitterness and resentment for your partner because they are not fulfilling your needs. But how will they know if you don't tell them?

A lot of men feel they can't be honest about wanting to be in an open relationship fearing the woman will want to cut ties with him. Or if they are honest about dating other women and not wanting a commitment at the time, the woman will prejudge them and end the friendship. The thing to remember is this, if you are straight up about who you are and what you want, the person can't fault you for anything down the line. This gives people the opportunity to make a conscious decision to deal with you or not. You never know what someone is willing to accept until you let your truth be known. And if they choose not to accept you for you, at least you saved you and them the headache before it got too deep. These are just some of the things you either learn through the courting process or things that courting will expose regardless of how much a person tries to camouflage his/her real intention and/or hidden agendas.

Old School Love

There was a time back in the days when a man took a woman on a date, simply to spend time with her, have a great time together and get to know her in the process. Sex after a date wasn't the motive. People have to get back to old school love. The love that was felt when Luther Vandross was playing in the background *"And it's so amazing, amazing, I can stay forever, forever"* or Gerald Levert was singing *"Baby hold onto me, see I'm a special kind, know that it's hard to find, told you a thousand times, baby hold on to me"*. It was the kind of love that made you proud to be with your partner. Where a man knew how to treat and respect a woman, and a woman knew how to treat a man as a King. It was a time when a man and woman were proud to show affection without feeling like they would be hated on or their relationship would be sabotaged. A time when a friend introduced you to another friend because they thought you would be a good match long term. It was the energy of love that kept these things going.

Courting should never stop, even when you are in an established relationship. Regardless if you are married for 15 years, engaged, dating for years or newly dating, you should always create situations to date and court your partner. People change over time mentally, physically and emotionally. Change is good and should be embraced and nurtured. When you are courting, you should be changing and growing together. You should be so in tune with each other that the lines of communication stay open, which lessens the possibility of growing apart or resenting each other down the line.

Tips to Courting

Everything comes to you at the right time, be patient and trust the process.

Ladies, allow a man to court you. The mentality of "I don't need a man" has to stop if you really do want one. If you're a boss, be with a boss and respect him as such. Men, take the time to invest in a woman you are interested in. Kisses on the cheek and forehead, asking someone out in person instead of text or phone, engaging in conversation that ask the important questions are all examples of the initial courting phase. Find out each-others interests and experience those things together. Most importantly, be honest about what you want.

In our early courting stages, we went out on dates and experienced each other in different environments. We went to sports bars, strip clubs, mountain climbing, brunch, car shows, picnics in the park and made food to the feed homeless. We established a bond from all angles and made sure no matter what we did we could have fun with each other. We attended government contracting classes together in order to see if that was an opportunity for business we could both pursue. While in those classes we cracked jokes and talked about people (petty I know) and made it fun while we learned another way to build together.

We also created what we called Truth Moments. If there was something we needed to tell the other person, or something we needed to get off our chest, one of us would call a truth moment. What this did was prepare the other person to listen to something that could potentially piss them off, but agreeing to discuss it instead of just reacting. For example, when we started dating I would tell my husband when my ex kept reaching out to me and sending gifts to my job trying to reestablish a relationship. I told him because we were friends and I never wanted him to feel uncomfortable if he ever found out any other way. It brought a certain level of respect to our friendship turned relationship and helped build trust because we were able to talk to each other about anything without being judged or without it leading to an all-out argument. I would call a truth moment when we were in the early stages of dating. I told my wife that people from my past were pissed at the fact that they would never have another chance with me and they could potentially try to sabotage our relationship. This gave my wife the upper hand so she would never be caught off guard or looking stupid if anyone tried to say anything to her. It gave her the confidence in knowing no one could ever say anything about her man that she didn't already know and could shut it down before it even got started. Truth moments early on let the cat out of the bag about our past relationships, fears and insecurities. But it gave us an opportunity to decide whether we wanted to deal with each other and whatever baggage we brought to the table. Everyone has baggage, the problem is they don't reveal it until they are forced to deal with it.

Another aspect of courting is environment. Find ways to spend time with a person in different situations. This will show you the different sides of a person and how they carry themselves. Is this person the same when you go have drinks or when you just go sit outside and talk? Is he/she consistent in their level of communication or did he/she start off calling and texting every day and a few months later you only hear from him/her every 2 or 3 days? Pay attention to the obvious. Remember the goal is to invest time in someone you can ultimately build with. If you see the person is not consistent early on (chances are he/she will not become consistent later), cut ties and keep it moving.

Try coming up with something you can both agree on that keeps the lines of communication open. Honesty is one of the biggest keys to courting because the whole point is to get to know the real person you're dealing with. You might decide to send each other texts to express something that you normally would feel uncomfortable expressing. It gives the person a chance to take it in and have a face-to-face discussion about it later.

Practice Courting

Think about how you would like to experience dating someone everyday for the rest of your life.

What would that look like? Where would you like to go and what would you like to do?

What questions would you ask?

What would you want to know about the person?

What would you want them to know about you?

•••

The Energy of Love

Intermission Chapter

" Love is Energy of Life"- Robert Browning

The most powerful energy in this universe is love. The one desire everyone has no matter age, race or economic background is the desire to love and be loved. We look for it in our relationships, in our parents and children, in our immediate families and even in our close friendships. But how often do we look for it within our self? We count on love to heal, build and create, but when it fails, the feeling and impact it has is almost as strong as experiencing the death of someone you love. Have you ever gone through a breakup and right after the breakup you found it hard to breathe? You try to catch your breath in between thoughts or tears but it's almost as if a shockwave came through and knocked the air out of you. Sometimes you feel physically sick for days, weeks or even months and the world doesn't feel the same. You don't want to see anybody happy or talking about their relationships. Every song you hear either makes you want to ball up crying or punch a wall. That is the power of the energy of love. It can make you see and experience life from its most beautiful space or it can leave you in a place of misery and despair.

Energy starts with you. A lot of times your energy is connected to how you feel about yourself. Think about a time when you were really feeling yourself. You might have gotten a new outfit to go out in, you know you looked good, got your hair done, got a fresh fade (haircut), had some money in your pocket and at that moment nothing could take you off course. You had confidence and an aura about yourself that others felt when you walked by. People gave you compliments like "Damn, you're looking good today or I love your energy." You got attention from the opposite sex that screamed "I wish my man/ woman looked like that". It wasn't just about looks; it was the energy that you gave off from how you felt about yourself. These gestures and compliments were manifested because of the confidence and swag you projected through your presence and demeanor. The love that you felt for yourself was felt by everyone who came in contact with you. People felt a strong positive energy through your presence and gave you that energy in return. People say even the most unattractive person can be attractive when they carry themselves with confidence. So what happened after receiving that attention? You started to feel even better about yourself, therefore attracting more like energy. There is a quote from the football great Deon Sanders that says "When you look good, you feel good, when you feel good you play good, when you play good they pay good". Everything you want to attract starts with the energy of loving yourself first.

Love Energy in Relationships

In a perfect world the more love you put out the more love you will receive, but we all know this is not a perfect world. When you are with the right person love should be easy right? So why do so many people say love is hard? There will always be challenges where love is concerned but when the energy is right, those challenges will be easier for you and your partner to face together.

Well what does love energy feel like in a relationship?

It's an energy that is encouraging and supportive and makes you feel like you want to be a better person. It's how you feel when you talk about how great your partner is with other people. It's that feeling you get when your partner consistently shows you he/she appreciates you. It's that feeling you get when your partner takes time to listen to you, cheer you on and boost you up when your spirits are low.

Love energy is a positive reaffirming reassuring flow two people have when they are in a healthy relationship. When people have this kind of energy in their relationship, they work through disagreements, they're inclined to see each other's point of view, respect each other's opinions, and they don't try to be the dominate voice during discussions or disagreements.

If you're in a relationship that is full of strife; arguments, disrespect, emotional, verbal and/or physical abuse, the energy in your relationship will be negative. A relationship like this can suck the energy out of you to the point where your personality begins to change and the success of your future is at risk.

We all know at least one person who has experienced this. He/she is no longer this smiling optimistic goal oriented person, they are stressed out and constantly worried and focusing on what is going wrong opposed to what to do to make things better.

Energy in relationships is a 2-way street. You cannot be a positive joyful person and deal with someone who is full of anger, spite or envy. You can't be an ambitious go-getter and deal with someone who is content with being unhappy. If you don't see an equal love energy transfer in your relationship, then it's time to re-evaluate your relationship. Happiness as an energy flow is something no one should ever compromise. A lot of times people stay in relationships thinking they can outlast unhappiness or change an unhappy person. The energy that it takes to try and change a mean or bitter person is often so overwhelming that it will leave you jaded toward love in the future.

The Energy of Your Thoughts

What you think about most, is what you will attract the most of in your life. When you focus on the things you desire and you believe with all your heart that you deserve those things, and act as if you already have it, the world will open up for you to receive those things depending on your thoughts and intentions. On the other hand, what is also true is, if you constantly focus on the negative, you will attract undesirable people and situations.

It's very important to pay attention to what you focus your attention on as well as what you talk to yourself about, we call that "self-talk". What are you saying to yourself when you have those "self-talk" moments? Are you sowing seeds of doubt or negativity in your own mind?

You have a responsibility to protect the energy of your thoughts by any means necessary. In a society filled with negativity and distractions, it's important to train yourself to dismiss negative thoughts. You have to be mindful of not only what you say to yourself and others, but how you say them. For instance, if you want to have a healthy relationship or want to find a partner to build with, you have to keep away from thinking or saying things like, "I'm never going to find anyone" or "I'm going to be single forever", or "these men/women aint shit." You cannot immerse yourself in TV or music that constantly shows a negative image of relationships because those images are impressed upon your subconscious. And this is how you will start to view and experience relationships.

We're not telling you to completely disassociate with whatever form of entertainment you choose, but you have to have balance. Speak what you want into existence. Say things like, "I know I'll be with the person I'm meant to be with", or "everything that has happened and is happening is shaping me to be my best self, now it's up to me to use it". Then put yourself in the environments and surround yourself with people who give off that same energy.

Practicing Love Energy

Take some time to practice loving yourself first. Start with looking in the mirror every day and complimenting yourself. Tell yourself that you are fearless and no matter what the day brings, you're going to "Beast Through Anything" – Jessie Lewis.

See yourself as a King or Queen and embrace the energy behind the title. You have the ability to pick up any energy you want and become that. So if you pick up an energy of fear, you will be a victim of fearful situations. Talk to yourself while you look in the mirror and remind yourself that you have everything it takes to get what you want; you just have to take the first step. Speak to your higher self, your God/Goddess, with confidence and conviction and declare what you want.

Make a conscious decision to extend love daily.

I tell my husband constantly how handsome he is and how proud I am for how hard he works to make our dreams come true. This motivates him even more to get out and grind for his family. Tell your spouse you're proud of him/her for something he/she has done. Speak life into each other. Tell him/her you recognize their efforts, determination and/or passion for the goals he/she trying to achieve. Simply tell your partner that you appreciate him/her.

Compliment a stranger (especially women, compliment another woman) daily. Support a family or friend's business and spread knowledge on things that you know are beneficial to others. These are the types of steps you can use to practice love energy. These actions help bring forth the type of energy you want to receive daily.

30 Day Energy Cleanse

Try this exercise for 30 days and watch how you become more clear about who you are, what you want and what you need in your life. After 30 days you will notice that you are attracting the things you truly desire.

• Fast on something that you may need to slow down on or give up altogether. When you're serious about this you won't have to think long about what you need to give up, be honest with yourself.

Ex. Give up meat, sex, sugar, dating, negative messages on tv, or non-productive conversations with others are just some examples.

Write down what you're giving up

• Meditate: Take 10 minutes every day preferably in the morning (you can afford to take 10 min out of your day), and practice these 3 techniques.

- For beginners, just start with sitting quietly for 10 min. You don't have to control or stop your thoughts or say anything. Just simply start with sitting with yourself in a quiet serene place and just be.

- To expand on this, spend 3 min focusing on the things you are grateful for. Visualize it and feel it. Think about being alive no matter what struggles you are faced with, because you know someone somewhere somehow has it worse than you. Or simply focus on being grateful for the ability to provide for your family.

Write down 3 things you are grateful for and focus on them for 3 minutes.

1.

2.

3.

- Now spend 3 minutes thinking about 3 things you want to come to pass in the next 6 months and list them below. The point of this is to think about what you want when you are already in a place of gratitude.

1.

2.

3.

- Lastly think of 3 things you can do each day out of love for yourself and/or for someone else. Doing something out of love when you are in this state only enhances the energy of receiving those things you want. List some things you can do for someone else.

1.

2.

3.

After 30 days evaluate your mood, your experiences and the results in things you did. You should find yourself in a more confident and fulfilled place making it easier to face challenges and make clear decisions that will ultimately be for your greater good.

••

CONSIDERATION

BLAC HEARTBEAT #2

1. careful thought, typically over a period of time.

"Within the hearts of man, loyalty and consideration are esteemed with success"- BLAC Heartbeat

Are you being considered in your relationship? In a healthy relationship you should always be looking for ways to keep the fire lit. You should be paying attention to the needs of your partner and together explore ways to keep the relationship alive and exciting.

Consideration in Relationships

This 2nd Heartbeat is what makes and breaks relationships. You became friends, you courted, now it's getting serious. Consideration allows both parties to make conscious decisions about agreeing to invest feelings, emotions, time, intimacy and even exchange monetary favors with each other. When you think of consideration in your relationship, think of consideration as a business agreement between you and your partner. Like we said in the previous chapter, you want to benefit from and be a benefit to the person you're involved with.

In our relationship our core values and vision for our future were in alignment. The consideration to invest in a relationship with one another was our agreement. To invest the time to grow and build with one another, to value the other person, to communicate and set goals together was the consideration. One major aspect of this agreement was the freedom to be ourselves. **You cannot be with a person you can't be yourself with**.

We worked with a couple who have been together over 10 years and are still in their early 30's, married and with children. Their friendship may have been in tact in their early stages of dating, but over time they grew apart due to lack of consideration. The man in the relationship (Reggie) is in a marriage with a women (Lisa) who does not fulfill his needs because he was never honest about who he is. Reggie is outgoing, ambitious and has a healthy sex drive but he started the relationship being the man he knew Lisa wanted (blue collar worker, someone who goes to church every Sunday, and satisfied with a basic lifestyle. Now he's battling with himself and his marriage.

See, Reggie married Lisa because she is beautiful, smart, family oriented and he knew she would be a good mother to their children. He didn't take into consideration that her personality was not what he truly wanted in a woman. She didn't stimulate him mentally and didn't encourage him to go for what he wanted in life. She was satisfied with a 9-5 job and a basic style of living. But Reggie dreamed of entrepreneurship and wealth. This lead Reggie to cheat throughout their entire relationship, resulting in a child outside of their marriage. Had this couple courted in the beginning, they may not have wasted so much time when it became obvious they were not happy with each other. Now children are involved and they're the ones who will be directly affected. Remember, be honest with yourself about who you are and what you want. Consider yourself first, then consider all who will be affected by your decisions.

Take a look at your relationship and determine what you and your partner need to consider in order to build a stronger unit.

Parenting

Before having a child an agreement can be made while you are currently in a relationship that identifies the responsibility of both parties. You can determine that if anything were to happen and the relationship ended, that instead of putting the child in the "system" and asking for child support, an agreement is made beforehand that specifies what the parents will contribute and how often. Child support that is agreed upon prior to taking it to court is an example of how to implement consideration in relationships when you decide to have children. When better to discuss it than when you are both in a good space with each other instead of battling and being vindictive.

Too often in our community we don't take into consideration what happens after we have children with someone. Which is why this information is so important. It puts you in position to really look at who you are dealing with and what could happen if it didn't work out. Especially when you have assets, most important asset being a child. How can you protect yourself and your children along the way? Simple contracts can save much time and money in the end. If you want to look into this further speak with a lawyer to get a legal understanding.

Blended Families

When two individuals come together and have children they bring into the relationship, consideration is a HUGE factor. Not only are the 2 individuals agreeing to invest in a relationship with each other, but the children are also a part of this agreement. When you bring children into a relationship, your first consideration should be, does this person have the potential to fully invest in and nurture your children. Because your children deserve the best from you and anyone you bring into their lives.

When making a decision to blend families, more than likely you both have already decided that this will be a long term relationship. One of the most important things to consider when incorporating children into relationships, is how you both want to parent the children.

Both parties have to be mindful that it's no longer an "I" thing, it's now a "WE" thing. This is where communication is going to be key (if you have trouble communicating early on, and attempt to blend families later on, you may run into some serious issues). Both individuals in the relationship have to be mature enough to let their guard down and come to a mutual agreement as to the role they will play in the children's lives. They have to determine if the man is going to take on the role as a father figure to her children and how to go about disciplining, or is he going to allow the child's mother to be the disciplinarian. What role does the woman play in the relationship with his kids? Will she be considered a mom figure or more of an extension to the family and let him handle the kids. How do you both want the family life to look?

These are important questions to ask and facts to consider because not being clear of each person's responsibility can damage and possibly end an otherwise good relationship.

Determine what things are important to you when it comes to your children. Think about not only what you want from your partner when it comes to being in your kids' lives, but what do the kids need at this time in their lives that your partner can provide. Have the conversations early on, clearly define what you both want, agree on a way of living, communicate constantly and remember that you are on the same team and the goal is to win together.

CONSIDER YOUR RELATIONSHIP A BUSINESS

Common Law Marriage

Let's jump into common law marriages which are very common in this day and age but only recognized in a few states. Many couples live together without being legally married and there's so many reasons why. Sometimes it's financial, children or they're just in love and don't want to be in separate households.

Common law marriages are usually established and identified when the couple lives together for a long period of time, portray their relationship in public as being husband and wife and/or have shown intention to get married. Sometimes the couples can have something as small as a car insurance policy together for a certain amount of time and the state considers them common law.

Consideration plays its role when it comes to common law marriages because most of the time when couples have lived together for a long period of time, they have either established joint bank accounts, combined or accumulated debt together or have joint assets. There may be situations where they have an agreement to do or not do something that they are not legally obligated to do.

For instance, both parties agree to split the bills. But your partner was unfaithful and you decide you are not paying anymore bills. Legally you were not obligated to pay bills, but once you two agreed on splitting them, a legal binding contract was established. So the bills are not being paid in full, the landlord comes after whomever is on the lease (your ex) but your ex comes after you in court because you did not hold up to your agreement of splitting the bills.

In these cases, agreements were made with both parties as to what they each agreed to invest into these relationships and what each person would get out of it. In those states where common law is recognized, if a break up were to happen, it would be similar to going through a divorce.

So if you are or think you are in a common law marriage, find out if your state recognizes common law marriages, and make sure you are clear on the agreements that have been established between you and your partner. Know what belongs to you and what belongs to them. Understand your monetary investments and understand your debts. Make sure you create verbal or paper contracts (preferably paper contracts that are notarized) that protect you from losing anything you've invested.

Personal Asset vs. Liability

In relationships and marriages asset considerations are highly recommended when you are looking to build together. Your partner first and foremost should be an asset to you and vice versa. When you are an asset to each other, look forward to a personal value increase. If you both are an asset to your relationship, then investing should be an easy win.

Ask yourself, is the person you're with an asset or liability to you and your relationship? How can you tell?

Assets

- Brings a smile and a sense of happiness to you when you are around him/her?
- He/she appreciates you and values you as a King or Queen
- He/she encourages you to be your best self

Liabilities

- Brings an instant frown to your face and you feel uneasy when he/she is around
- Is physically, mentally and/or emotionally abusive
- Is financially irresponsible

That's how to tell if the person you're involved with is an asset or liability.

If you're serious about having a romantic relationship with someone you can build wealth with, you have to know the differences between assets and liability. As in the business world you keep assets and get rid of liabilities.

Building Business Assets Consideration

An asset is simply something that has value or can be exchanged for cash. When considering what to invest in with your partner, be sure to determine what you both expect to get out of the investment.

Some examples of assets couples can invest in are investment products (ex. stocks, money market accounts, and savings account), real estate (ex. Commercial property, rental property, flipping houses, or purchase a property to live in and sell it when the market value increases), flipping cars, selling clothes, selling items on amazon, writing a book, selling hair supplies, even selling used electronics or furniture and the list can go on.

When we decided to build assets together we looked into what we both were interested in and what we knew would yield quick profits. We invested in a few companies that were on the rise and companies we spent a lot of money with. We spent time together doing our research to make sure we were making good investments and we purchased stock with those companies that we agreed was worth the investment. After about 6 months, we cashed out on some of those stocks, purchased more with other companies and used some of the profit to start our foreclosure cleanout business Castle Cleanout. We also purchased stock shares for our son when he was born. We decided on companies that were long standing and not too risky because we knew we could keep that money in those stocks until he becomes old enough to cash out.

Thank us later son!

The first step is to find out what you both are interested in. When you have a mutual interests and realize you can make money from it, the process and decisions become a lot less complicated. You're excited about the possibilities and you want to put your best foot forward. It brings you and your partner closer and increases the value in your relationship.

On top of the emotional and physical bond, now you are adding another dynamic that will propel your relationship to new heights. It gives your relationship another sense of purpose. You and your partner are more conscious of the decisions you make, because now your money and investments are on the line, and no one wants to screw that up.

Consideration on Assets and Profits

When entering into an agreement to build assets with your partner here's a few things that should go into the consideration process.

- What do we expect to get out of the investment?
- Be clear on what percentage of the profit you both get individually.
- Make sure you both are satisfied with what you could potentially get out of the deal based on what you put in.
- Evaluate where you and your partner are financially and what financial goals each of you have going forward.
- Come up with a list of some assets that you both can potentially invest in at this point in your relationship.
- Set a date and list some options that you would like to invest in when that time comes.

Then get to work!

For example, you both may agree to open a joint savings account and put away $100 a week each. With the goal being to use the accumulated saving to purchase a rental property after one year.

List 5 potential investment opportunities for you and your partner now.

1.

2.

3.

4.

5.

List 5 potential investments for you and your partner 5 years from now.

1.

2.

3.

4.

5.

• •

APPRECIATION

BLAC HEARTBEAT #3

1. the recognition and enjoyment of the good qualities of someone or something.

2. to refer to an increase in any type of asset

"Don't forget a person's greatest emotional need is to feel appreciated"- H. Jackson Brown

Baby I appreciate you! When was the last time you heard this from your partner?

When you appreciate someone you are thankful for the things he/she does for you and the good things he/she brings to your life. Can you identify specific qualities about your mate that make you appreciate him or her?

King Donte

I appreciate my wife on so many levels. I appreciate the fact that she is non-judgmental and gives me honest feedback when I put an outrageous idea on the table, and I have a lot of those. I appreciate that she supports and pushes me, she is always there to build me up opposed to tear me down the way I've been done in past relationships. I appreciate the fact that she believes enough to let me be the man she knows I am. I mean my list of appreciations go on and on.

And I let her know how much I appreciate her, by the things I do, not solely by the things I say. That's how you show someone you love you appreciate them.

Queen Tiffany Geselle

I appreciate my husband and I make it my mission to show him daily. He is my not only my biggest supporter in anything I desire to do but he goes out of his way to make my life easier in every way. He always introduces me to new and exciting experiences and makes sure our lives never has a dull moment. I have learned about love, life and living your dreams through his confidence in knowing we can have whatever we desire in life if we work together.

Appreciation is a fundamental element of a strong healthy relationship and it will compel partners to constantly look for ways to show it. From the grand (buying your partner a big ticket item) to a loving gesture (an unexpected passionate kiss followed by whispering the words, "I appreciate you in so many ways).

When you appreciate someone, you care about their feelings in every aspect of the relationship. The worse feeling in the world is being in a relationship where you are putting your all in, yet you're left feeling unappreciated. Feeling unappreciated will cause bitterness and resentment within a relationship. It will cause a lopsidedness within the relationship and it'll be hard to carry out any of the other tasks because you'll stop seeing that person as a partner. Stop, think, ask yourself when was the last time you told your partner you appreciated him/her?

This is important because after our example of appreciation in relationships and business, you will see that practicing this from here on out will raise your consciousness, build your confidence and give you boosts of energy to keep the relationship exciting. We kept consciousness in mind as we articulate the Five BLAC Heartbeats. Appreciation, being by far the most popular, plays a big part in defining the value in your relationships and business investments.

Appreciation in Relationships

Through BLAC Heartbeat we have discussed relationships and dating with thousands of black women and men. The one common issue that has been brought up during these discussions, was men and women feeling unappreciated in their relationship. Women are feeling unappreciated when giving their all emotionally in a relationship but those feelings are not being reciprocated. Men are feeling unappreciated when they are doing everything to make a woman happy, but she still finds a reason to be upset while not recognizing or acknowledging his efforts.

It's natural for a person to seek solace somewhere else if they are not getting it from the person they love. It's not fair to you or your spouse to remain in a relationship that is not full of gratitude for the other person. If you want a relationship to work, learn how to put the small petty things to the side and focus on why you are with the person you're with. What is it about the person you're with that brings you pleasure? Try to give each other what you need to avoid having to search for it somewhere else.

Imagine a relationship where you focused on how and what you could do to make sure your partner feels appreciated every time you were in contact with them or in their presence. Usually what will happen is your partner will feel so good about themselves that they will put forth even more effort to satisfy you. Now you're in a cycle of powerful and positive energy that continues to circulate. It almost feels like a friendly competition of who's going to outdo the other in finding ways to make each other smile.

Are you wasting time with someone, especially a partner who doesn't appreciate you? Be real with yourself and your situation. It's not difficult to see that you are in a relationship or situationship with someone who has no interest in building you up or building with you. If you put your all into a relationship than be sure in knowing that you deserve that same amount of attention in return. If you settle for less, you are telling the world you don't feel you deserve better.

"We All Get What We Tolerate"- Tony Robbins

Love Languages

My wife and I really connected when we discovered each-others love language. We both read The Five Love Languages before we met so we were able to discuss it and clearly tell each other what our individual love language was. To truly understand how to appreciate your partner all you need to do is understand their love language. Everyone has one love language that is more prevalent to them than the others. Do you know your partners love language? Do you know yours?

We realized in order to recognize someone's love language just pay attention to how they express their love toward you. If they always compliment you, they more than likely get off on getting compliments. If they like to touch you and be near you, then they may yearn to be touched and have that attention as well.

Let's explore these languages of love so you can better identify how to interpret your partner's love language in a way he/she can best receive your messages of appreciation. It'll also allow you to take a look at yourself and determine which one resonates with you the most. You can apply this to your relationships, children, friends etc.

Not in any particular order the 5 love languages include **Words of Affirmation, Gifts, Physical Touch, Quality Time**, and **Acts of Service**. Have you ever heard the phrase "It's the little things that count"? Well once you define your partners love language, you will be in a better position to do the small things that make them feel appreciated. There are so many simple ways to express these love languages if you put forth the effort and think outside the box. Here are some examples

- **Words of affirmation**- write notes on a sticky telling him/her how much you love them, how amazing they are, how you are proud of them. Say things like "You are the best looking man/woman I've ever seen."

Place the sticky notes all around the house where you know he/she will see them.

- **Gifts**- know what he/she likes. Buy tickets to a football game or concert, buy a card from the store and their favorite candy, write a note in the card and leave it where he/she can find it or give it to them on your next date.

- **Physical touch**- Give him/her a massage or rub on their head and temple while you both are laying down watching a movie. Grab her butt in the kitchen. Grab his face and kiss him passionately at random times in random places.

- **Quality time and Acts of service**- Make food to take to the homeless or start an activity in the community. Workout together, cook together, make plans to enjoy each-others company.

These are just a few fun examples of how to implement the love languages. If you pay attention to your partner, through actions or words they'll tell you what they like.

Appreciation in Business

You can easily see how appreciation in relationships transfer over to appreciation in business. In business, when someone refers to appreciation, they are talking about the value or increase in value of a person or object. For instance, if you and your partner purchased land 5 years ago for $10k and today it's worth $20k, the increase in value over the 5 years is the appreciation. The $10k profit that you and your partner both made, would definitely make you appreciate and respect each other and your relationship on a whole other level. See how this appreciation concept goes hand in hand.

When I met my husband he owned a valet company and at the time it wasn't doing well. When I came into the picture as his partner, we strategically made friends with people who owned clubs, bars, restaurants and event halls because we knew they would need the valet service at some point. He hired a crew and trained them, while I secured the contracts. I took care of the paperwork and communication, while he handled the ground work and made sure the business ran smoothly. Although we did not have an exact amount that the company would earn in the first few months, we knew the potential to make a sizable profit every week and we agreed to split it.

You see, my husband is a hustler with a combination of street and book smarts (I call him an intellectual ratchet). I'm a person who is great with contracts and making deals. We knew that if we both played our parts, by focusing on what we were good at individually, we would make a strong team, running a strong company. I believed in him and saw his ambition and his drive, so making the decision to go into business with him was easy. This alone allowed me to put my best foot forward and use my skills to catapult this business to the next level. Within the first 2 weeks we made all of our investment money back and some. It was all appreciation (profit) going forward and gave us the opportunity to expand.

The investment in our relationship was in each other. Believing in the other person enough to put your dreams in their hands and allowing it to increase the value of your relationship is what builds a strong unit. What's better than creating a financially free life with the person you want to spend your life with?

Benefits of Appreciation

As my appreciation (love and value) for my wife grew, the appreciation (value) of our company grew. Me showing my appreciation motivated her to continue to do what she does best because she is not doing it in vain. See how they both go together. Appreciation builds value in love and wealth.

When you are in a relationship where both parties show appreciation toward one another, you establish a bond and an overall healthy relationship. But more so it places a **higher value** on you and your partner. When you are constantly shown appreciation in your relationship, the feeling that you have is reflected in your energy. Your self-confidence is on 100, you recognize your worth and you put yourself on a higher pedestal.

When you are appreciated and when you appreciate someone, you are exhibiting that feeling of gratitude. When you make profits off of your investments, you feel gratitude. It's the law of attraction, what you think and feel will continue to come to you. Continue to appreciate and feel grateful and watch how things continue to unfold.

Appreciation Worksheet

List three things you appreciate about your partner

1.

2.

3.

List three ways he/she is showing his/her appreciation to you

1.

2.

3.

What are your love languages?

What is your partner's love language?

How can you show him/her appreciation through their love language?

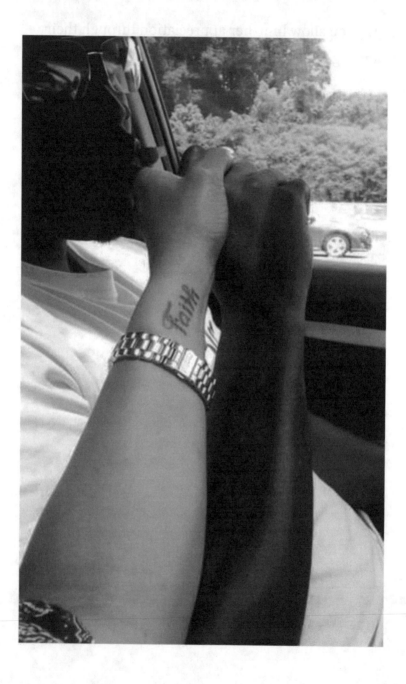

•••

Let's Talk About Sex

Bonus

"The sexual desire is the most powerful desire. It stimulates, develops imagination..."

Napoleon Hill

You've just been opened up to what appreciation should look like and how it will benefit you. You should be thinking and acting on your partners love language and now it's time to dive into the art of sex.

Why were black women made so perfect? Soft, sexy, big, small, tall, short, thick, slim, brown or light, you all have one thing in common, you are a GOD. Yes the black woman is a GOD and it's about time you get acknowledged and treated as such. Take pride in your role on this earth and know that without you the human race does not exist. Without your natural wisdom the black man has no guidance. It's important for the sake of mankind that all women get in tune with their spiritual power inside their body, also known as Chakras. There are 7 main chakras that represent the centers in our body in which energy flows through. Women need to know how to balance all chakras in order to build and maintain mental and emotional strength. The sacral chakra holds the energy of sex, sensuality, intimacy, emotions, pleasure and connection (research chakras on google to find how to balance all chakras). Some ways to balance your sacral chakra is by eating oranges, doing yoga, and releasing past emotional and sexual experiences. Get in tune with your sexual energy as you have the power to make heaven or hell on earth.

Pay close attention to this section as it will encourage you to understand sex as a building block for wealth, understand the male in all his imperfections, and let go of what you thought you knew about sex.

We must promote monogamy and strong unions if we want positive change to happen in our communities.

We'll be the first to say most people love the act of sex but many people don't understand its power. You should have sex two to three times a day, as sex is one of the keys to success and we'll explain how. The sexual positions, emotional feelings, and who you choose to have sex with plays a major role in the manifestation of wealth. In one of our favorite books Think and Grow Rich, Napoleon Hill talked about Sexual Transmutation and how having sex can bring your thoughts to life. Transmutation means to change something into another form. So in sex transmutation you are using the blissful energy you feel from sex and transferring it into whatever your desire is. If you focus your thoughts on what it is you want while having intercourse you will bring that desire into existence. For instance, your goal may be to purchase a home. If you and your partner both envision the home while you're having sex, think about it in detail, see every aspect of the home and use the energy of passion, love and ecstasy that attaches itself to whatever you are thinking about with your partner to brings life to the thought.

Sex with the right person will invoke the energy needed to knock down any task, goal or challenge you have to face. Have you ever felt liberated after having some crazy good sex? It's important for women to be sexually satisfied often. The sexual energy in women is setup different than men. Sex (not just sex but great sex) is necessary for women because when a woman is in tune with her body emotionally and spiritually she can reach her genius (when she is partnered with the right person).

Everyone we interviewed stated sex was at the top of the list when it came to dating and relationships. Why? Because its human nature to be sexually attracted to someone and desire intercourse. Most guys are taught to desire women at such an early age with society glorifying the idea that being with a woman or multiple women makes them a man! Young ladies get a lesson in sex as early as age 11 or 12 when they receive their menstrual cycle. Sex is learned early but very rarely taught in a way that allows people to understand its benefits if they respect the power of sex and go about it the right way.

So I'm sitting here having a bowl full of fresh baked apple pie, topped with butter pecan ice cream. The way the cool creamy pecan smooth texture combines with the hot flakey brown sugary crust and cinnamon infused apple filling hits my tongue, my taste buds go crazy, this has to be as good as love making, I say to myself. The way the dopamine is erupting in my brain has me on a natural high, almost the same way sex does. Sex can become an addiction just like drugs or any controlled substance when people take advantage of and abuse them. So it's important to have emotional and mental balance when choosing to engage in sexual acts so that you are not constantly chasing a high that will never be totally fulfilled.

Sex played such a huge role in the success of many of the wealthiest people on the planet. These people learned how to use sex to their advantage by channeling the energy to bring their dreams into reality. We want to touch on intercourse and its affects, how to have an intellectual orgasm, masturbation vs oral sex and how faking it is not good for the ladies. We will also touch on why men and women cheat.

What is Considered Sex? Physical Vs Mental

Sex is the physical act of bodies and souls coming in contact and intertwining as one. It happens via intercourse, kissing, hugging, touching and masturbating one another, as well as oral sex. Sex can also be mental stimulation when the souls and thoughts of all parties are on the same wave length. We often speak about having a mental orgasm and how important it is for couples or people dating to experience this before being intimate sexually. So what is a mental orgasm, and have you ever had sex with someone mentally? Mental stimulation occurs when two people are in sync and on the same vibration mentally. They elevate one another, through motivational affirmations, sexy conversations, physical appearance, luxurious or relaxing environments. Most people get their first mental stimulation from physical appearance. When men see women they consider attractive, naturally they are engaged because men are visual creatures. When some women see attractive men they are more likely to give those guys more attention than the guy who is less physically attractive.

Sex with Multiple Partners and its Affects

It is said that sex is energy, and if used properly can manifest and save lives. What people might not know is, we lose a part of ourselves any time we have sex with multiple people in a short period of time. This is because sex is a spiritual act and when it's not with someone you have a connection with, you take on that person's energy and the energy of everyone they've slept with. You take on their pain and trauma, their violations and insecurities and a part of them is left with you just as a part of you is left with them. When two people are not aware of the fact that they are sharing energy during sex then anything is liable to be transferred between them that can be harmful to one or both parties. Some women become emotional and carry so much pain after having sex with a guy because the guy's intent may have been no good and he might have had a bad spirit. You literally take a part of the other person's personality, so make sure you know who you lay down with. But when people are in agreeance with having a true sexual experience they will form an alliance and use sex to carry out any goal. People who are getting down with multiple people can use it to his/her advantage, how? Well like we said when the energy is on the same frequency sex can elevate you and all those involved. Reason being is because the more people involved with the same intention and like energy sex can create a powerful unification. Everyone involved must be aware of the participation to the activities in the bedroom and feel comfortable with the situation. Each person involved can create their thoughts, combine them with the thoughts of the other participants and use that energy to bring those thoughts to life.

Masturbation vs Oral Sex

Is masturbation good for relationships and is having oral sex a must? For most men masturbation is a favorite past time. Can too much of it be destructive to your relationship and/or to the progression of your life? Yes, fewer ejaculations from masturbation proves better focus and helps accomplish projects and boosts the ability to make quick concise decisions. When you minimize masturbation you conserve energy, regulate hormones, and your emotions and focus are aligned. Men, the body and mind knows the difference between intercourse and masturbation. With intercourse you receive a healthy dose of oxytocin and testosterone. With masturbation you mostly receive dopamine which will give you a natural high, but will not liberate you. Especially ladies, don't masturbate as much (not at all if you don't have to). Make sure when you have sex you get an orgasm and channel the energy toward your path to wealth.

Oral sex has been one of life's greatest exercise. How many people can really say they don't enjoy oral sex? Where does oral sex fall in line with manifesting wealth? We pass along energy back and forth when we simply touch or have our minds set on the same thoughts. Intercourse is by far the best way to transmute thoughts into reality (sex transmutation). Oral stimulation works similarly by taking control of your thoughts while in the act. Couples especially need to practice oral sex not just as acts of appreciation, but as a way to propel each other to the next level of self-confidence. Think of oral sex as a way to grow together sexually. Again we speak on these topics from a standpoint of being with a trustworthy committed partner. When you are secure in your relationship oral sex should come as easy and as often as sex does. To taste the natural juices of one another infuses and enhances the bond between two people engaged in sex. The key to oral sex is appreciation. You are agreeing to an act in which you are in control of pleasing your partner. When you perform oral sex on your partner make sure you are totally present in the act. It's not just a sexual experience, it's an energy transfer. You're down there doing your thing, they are giving off an energy of sensual pleasure, you get excited because you understand how good you are making them feel and in turn you feel motivated to keep making them feel good. Energy transfer.

We suggest giving fellatio during intercourse as foreplay intensifies the energy. Foreplay should be done in every sexual performance to get the juices flowing before the act itself. If you're a person who does not like to give or receive oral sex, let that be known in the beginning while dating. Because to some people it is a very important part in keeping a relationship exciting and could potentially be a deal breaker if not discussed up front. Don't be afraid to have these conversations. It's not embarrassing or inappropriate. It's mature and understandable.

Why Faking Orgasms is a NO NO!!!

When a woman ejaculates a sweet healing nectar is produced that is literally a healing potion. It may sound weird but when you understand the power of a woman and her body you will understand why faking an orgasm is a no no. Women need mental stimulation and sexual expression in order to induce orgasms that can change the course of their life. Orgasms for women is a force that brings forth the creativity needed to solve problems and come up with new innovative ideas. She's able to think from a higher than normal functioning brain. It is critical for women to receive orgasms from both mental and sexual pleasure. It brings her to a frequency that aligns with the universal energy of instant manifestation, it's the art of sex transmutation. The juices from her ejaculation is a liquid remedy for the person who is able to experience the ecstasy with her. It is a spiritual experience because the woman is a spiritual being and when used in its most natural state (sex) it can change the course of everything known to man. So ladies make sure you get yours. If you are not getting an orgasm most times you have sex, tell your partner what you need to get you there. Let him know what turns you on or how to get you excited.

Why Do Men Cheat?

Men naturally have more of a sexual appetite than women. And instinctively have a desire to procreate. So after speaking and interviewing several black men we found these to be the top 3 reason why men cheat.

Insecurity, selfishness, and lack of satisfaction.

**Insecurity**. Men have insecurities just like women and most men have a past they are not proud of. When men get cheated on and disrespected by women it causes them to lose trust going forward in dating and relationships. It can create a lack of self-confidence and a feeling of being unattractive or not good enough. The result is a man hopping around from woman to woman looking for someone to boost his confidence and make him feel good about himself. He needs support from a woman patient enough to deal with his issues.

When it comes to insecurity we think of our client Ralph, who is legally married, and has been fighting demons all throughout child hood that caused him to develop insecurities that he couldn't shake in his adult life. His insecurities about his looks, finances etc. lead to abusing drugs and running through women as a way to cover up the pain. Having a partner who understands his dilemma and who is not selfish enough to not pour alcohol on his wound is necessary. To deal with a man like our client, the woman herself can't be in a place of turmoil. She would need to be in a confident and progressive state herself to balance out the energy this type of man will bring.

Selfish. Some men have big egos and a competitive nature. These types of men can look at being with women as a sport. Is this right, of course not, but it is the honest truth. Some men since they were able to have sex, have been on a mission to smash (have sex with) as many women as they can. The fact is boys have that mentality, but when the boys become men they are supposed to leave childish acts behind. Stemming from activities in their past some men take a little longer to adjust and mature. If a man is not ready to settle down and show signs of indecisiveness, ladies please believe him. See, the thing about selfish men is they can have a steady situation, good woman, good relationship etc. Yet because it's all about them, being with multiple women feed their selfish egos. Ladies never try changing a man like this, if he doesn't align with your destiny write his ass off.

Lack of Satisfaction. Ladies the reality is you hold a lot of the cards. Let's be honest people usually play their best cards early on. Over time those faces you put on fade away, and the true face is revealed. Although men come off tough and masculine there is always a feminine balance that is needed. Men do need emotional and mental support, on top of the physical. Sometimes women get comfortable after being with a guy for a period of time. They aren't paying attention to his needs as much and think the good woman card solves everything. There are a lot of good women, but a damn good woman knows how to remain a lady and maintain her man's attention.

Sometimes you have to go back to the basics (courting) and revisit what made you and him so attracted to each other. Stroke his ego, maintain your sexiness, give him space when needed, talk to his spirit, and create a scene to which you play out his fantasies. Remember mental stimulation is just as important as physical stimulation and should receive the same amount of effort.

Why Do Women Cheat?

If you hear about a couple who broke up due to someone cheating, who is the person you would think is the wrongdoer? The man right? What if we told you that women cheat just as much as men, they're just sometimes better at not getting caught. We've had conversations with hundreds of women who gave us a few common reasons as to why women cheat and you'd be surprised at how simple it could be to prevent such an unfortunate circumstance.

__Feeling Unappreciated.__ While men are more visual, most women are more emotional. Women are nurtures and when they decide to entertain a relationship or commit to someone she usually makes it her job to nurture her partner. It's almost a godly role she takes on in the sense of wanting to guarantee her partner is always satisfied and taken care of. Sometimes it's through cooking and cleaning, satisfying him sexually, staying sexy or keeping up her physical appearance, taking care of the children, encouraging him to make the best moves or being his comfort zone. The amount of time and energy it takes to maintain a relationship and be a good partner can be exhausting and draining if it's with someone who doesn't appreciate you. At times women get caught up in relationships and lose themselves because they pour so much into the relationship and spend so much energy on that person without getting nurtured in return. A woman feeling neglected, ignored or disrespected can lead them right into the arms of someone else who is giving them the attention and appreciation they are yearning for.

To combat any chance of your woman feeling unappreciated it's simple, appreciate her. Acknowledge what she does on a daily basis to provide for you or make you into a better person. If she cooks you dinner, give her a massage afterwards. If she takes care of the kids, take the kids off her hands and send her to get her nails done and relax for the day. Words can play a major role if it's sincere, so initiate conversations that are dedicated to you finding out how she is feeling, what's on her mind and how much you love and appreciate her. Make it so that she gets all the attention she needs at home so anyone else that would try to come into the picture wouldn't have a chance.

To Get Even. Everyone knows the R. Kelly song "When a woman's fed up, no matter how you feel, there aint nothing you can do about it" Women are strong, we know this as a fact. And in relationships women tend to forgive their partners when they make mistakes. But if a mistake keeps occurring, or cheating is involved, regardless of how strong a woman is, some will stay in an unhealthy situation and deal with the mistreatment while others might stay but look for a way to get even or get out. She may start dressing sexy, going out more, ignoring you, talking down to you or giving someone else flirtatious attention. If you cheat on a woman you can guarantee that she will lose some respect for you if not all. Some women may look to have sexual contact with someone to get even and some women may entertain another person with conversation and time spent. This to her says "I'm going to make him feel the way he made me feel" or "since he did this to me let me see what else is out there".

So to not put your woman in a situation to which she feels she has to get even, be sincere in your actions by showing her you are open to doing whatever it takes to make the relationship work. Give her time and be patient. Answer questions and have open communication about whatever needs to be discussed but you have to agree to listen. Also, if you know you are not satisfied with your partner be honest with yourself and understand the reason why you're not happy. Ask yourself this question, if nothing about this situation ever changed could you be with this person and be happy or are you settling?

Mental or Sexual Dissatisfaction. When women are aroused mentally their sex drive will increase because of their desire to reach a euphoric experience like an orgasm. That feeling of ecstasy resonates with the body and spirit so much that if a woman's needs are not being met her subconscious mind will take over and possibly take advantage of an opportunity to have her needs met else-where.

If a man wants to turn a woman on mentally and keep her in tune with him he just needs to pay attention to her verbal and physical signs and that will tell you what she needs. Sometimes women won't come right out and say what they want or need simply because they want you to put in the time and energy to know them to the point where they don't have to give off signs and you do things effortlessly. For mental satisfaction talk to her about the future, life, love, wealth or whatever her interests are. Keep her engaged. People are innately attracted to positive people and positive energy. Keep the conversation positive and genuine sometimes seductive, sometimes aggressive. Just like in the bedroom when you want to be dominate and aggressive because you know what you want, take that same approach in pleasing her mentally. Women love a man that is confident and knows what he wants and includes her in his plans and decisions.

How Having Sex with Your Partner Brings About Success!

Most people spend their entire adult lives going through sex partners and encountering sexual experiences that serve them no purpose besides that moment of satisfaction. With knowledge comes opportunity. We have just revealed why and how sex can be used to manifest and create prosperity for you and your partner. Ladies this should help you in determining if someone is worthy of your nectar. Remember that you are the spirit of all living things. That means that you have the power in you and in your most precious parts that can cure, create and destroy life. If you want your partner to enjoy giving you oral sex, and get all the benefits from powerful orgasms, eat right and take care of your body. Eat alkaline fruits and vegetables daily, pineapples and mangos are good snacks that can help your juices smell and taste sweet. Men understand the power of the "yoni". It is up to you to protect it, nurture it, respect it and please it. Be choosy in who you share yourself with because choosing the wrong person/ people can leave their negative energy on you from their past trauma. Instead choose someone who straddles you mentally and makes you feel motivated when you are together. Know what both of your goals are, agree on what you both want to manifest and get your thoughts in alignment with one another. Get into sexual partnerships where you can create your own wealth through sex transmutation.

• •

TRUST

BLAC HEARTBEAT #4

1.   *firm belief in the reliability, truth, ability or strength of someone or something*

"No Trust, No Us"- BLAC Heartbeat

What is the most common issue that causes relationships to fail?

If you ask this question to anyone who has ever been in a relationship, 9 times out of 10 the answer would be infidelity or finances. As far back as we can go in human history, there has been a mindset and culture that says in many monogamous relationships men seek to be with other women, while the woman is usually faithful and with one man.

The culture made this acceptable even though morally we know it's not right. People have the right to choose what works for them in their relationships, as long as all parties involved are in agreeance. What's not right is the dishonesty in relationships resulting in things like the spread of disease and the breakup of families. Let's explore the decision to trust in relationships/business and the consequences of breaking trust, in hopes to bring light to a powerful tool that can create long lasting relationships or damage them to the point of no return.

Learned Behavior

Giving up limiting fear based beliefs is not always easy but necessary if you want a successful relationship.

Our community is plagued with a lack of trust and some of that stems from the generational cycle of fatherless children. When children feel abandoned or unprotected by their parent(s) it's the first experience on the path to mistrust. Often a child will feel if his/her own parent, the person who helped create them doesn't have their best interest at heart, why should they trust anyone else to. As children get older, they carry those experiences into their relationships and then adapt to their environment.

Because of our environment we were forced to watch out for people and possible hidden agendas that people may have. Where we come from, today's friend can be tomorrow's enemy. Trust has literally put people in the grave.

Even though trust comes hard for most people, we can't live our lives in fear of trusting because of our past experiences.

In our relationship we both knew loyalty was one of the many characteristics we looked for in a person and loyalty breeds trust. We had to be fearless enough to open the door to trusting each other as we proved ourselves deserving of it. We had to break the generational cycle of unhealthy relationships, single motherhood, absent fathers and split up families that contributed to our fear of trust.

Decision to trust

- What does it take for you to develop trust in your relationship?
- Have you identified your trust issues?
- Is it possible to rebuild trust with your partner (people) after you have been hurt or disappointed by him/her?
- Do you trust the person you are currently with?
- Can you trust their judgement?

These are some of the questions most people ask when discussing trust in relationships, and honestly, these are some questions you should ask yourself when evaluating your relationships. The one answer to all of those questions is TRUST IS A DECISION, NOT AN OBLIGATION. Do not allow people to make you feel like you are obligated to put your trust in them. Let people prove themselves in order to earn your trust. It's important that you be a loyal and trustworthy person if you expect that in return.

Don't let past experiences destroy the potential of a great relationship. Use your past experiences to make you better in the skill of detecting untrustworthy people and get the hell out of dodge sooner than later. Choose to embrace people who have exhibited their trustworthiness.

Trust in Relationships

Trust should be non-negotiable in a relationship. If you feel you can't or don't trust your partner, there's usually a good reason why. If that feeling of mistrust persists (even after talking to your partner) then we recommend you look for a way to exit this relationship.

Full trust should be earned, but some trust should be given. Some people start their relationships by saying, "I'm going to trust you until you give me a reason not to." We don't recommend this because trust should be rated on a scale. The more a person proves themselves trustworthy the higher they rise on the "trust scale". Being able to fully trust someone should be the highest point on the scale.

A confident man creates the feeling of trust with a woman. A secure woman creates a feeling of trust with a man.

No one wants to be in a relationship with someone they don't trust or who doesn't trust them. Many times we see women and men who go through their partner's phones, emails and personal belongings. We have one suggestion for you, **STOP NOW!** It's a direct reflection of your insecurity and a lack of self-confidence. This may be a reality check for most. But if you are this person, we want you to step back and take a look at yourself. We want you to recognize the underlying issues that are making you feel insecure and address them so you can live as the God/Goddess you are meant to be.

Once you begin questioning your partner's intentions and commitment, it can take significant effort to save the relationship. If you are with someone who has betrayed your trust, and you can't forgive and move past it, you should consider separating from that person to save you both the misery of living a life walking on eggshells. We should be free and happy with the person we choose to be with. Not constantly thinking about or checking for what they may be doing wrong.

Another huge issue we have found in the category of trust is gossiping about your partner to other people. This is something that can destroy a relationship quicker than you can blink. Gossiping about your partner and speaking down about them to others is a form of betrayal. You cannot expect to build trust and security in your relationship when you run to everyone telling them your business. Nor can you expect for those people to respect your partner when all you do is talk bad about them. Try to minimize the negative conversations you have about your partner and your relationship. Some people don't want to see you happy and some people thrive on your downfalls so keep your personal business in house. If you are in an abusive or unhealthy relationship and your safety or wellbeing is being compromised seek help immediately.

It's a beautiful feeling to have trust in your relationships. It all goes back to the previous points we've made. When someone is your friend, you court. They should consider you and your feelings, they should appreciate you, and when these things are in play it makes it a whole lot easier to put your trust in them. You feel comfortable with them because you know they have your best interest at heart and you can be all of yourself without being judged. You feel as though you have a partner in life and you are not alone when striving every day to survive in this cruel world. It gives strength to your relationship in turn building you up as a unit.

If you've been hurt by someone and you want to trust them again, and they genuinely want to make it work, here is a suggestion, go back to the basics. Start from the beginning. Become friends again and start courting. Get to know each other again from where you are now. Get to understand them. And allow the relationship to naturally take its course.

Trust in Business

We did a survey and asked some couples who have been married for 1 to 3 years if they have a trust account. Then we asked some couples that have been married for over 10 years if they have a trust account. Who do you think has the trust account?

What is a trust account? How does it work when it comes to business and/or business with your life partner?

In its simplest form, a trust account is an account where funds are held to achieve a specific purpose or goal. If you place money in an account for a specific bill every month or for disbursing money in installments to a person or place, this is considered a trust account. The person or entity (usually banks) that holds the money in the account, or the account holder, is considered the trustee. This person is responsible for who administers the trust. So be very careful when you set up will's and trust accounts who you choose to be your trustee. The person or entity receiving the monies is considered the trust beneficiaries.

When it comes to trust in relationships and business, a couple who has children would want to consider setting up a trust for their family (consult an attorney). What this does is provide **security** to the children or family members upon the death of the individual who set up the trust. The couple will put a certain amount into an account and if something happens to them, the children will receive money each month coming from the trust account. This is important because it allows the children and family members to not suffer financially if an unexpected tragedy occurs.

We can also talk about irrevocable trusts. This is the type of trust that once established cannot be changed or terminated without the consent of the beneficiary. Since it cannot be changed, it is of upmost importance to have the trust setup very carefully and more important to carefully choose who will be the trustee, or administrator of the funds upon your death. Anyone can be the trustee of an irrevocable trust, including, and who should be your spouse. This means you have to truly trust your spouse in order to know that they will carry out your wishes. If you pass on, will they disburse the money or property in the way that you requested?

An irrevocable trust can also be in the form of an estate (real estate property). If you make your spouse the sole beneficiary of an estate, then that property held in a marital trust avoids estate tax. If you are not married, the properties trust can be passed to multiple beneficiaries without estate tax.

The trustee can only use the property the way it is outlined in the trust. So it's important that you are specific in your requests on how you want the property or money used and managed, especially since it's almost impossible to change it after it's been established.

Conclusion of Trust

Back to the original question, who do you think has the trust account?

- The couple of 10 years of course. They've had a trust account from the moment they started investing and producing profits. A trust account shows they trust each other enough to agree on how their assets should be handled upon death. It shows they are dedicated to being with one another for a lifetime.

- The couple that have been married about three years don't have a trust because they have no assets (living in an apartment or no purchased home), both work a 9 to 5 and their debt almost exceeds their income. The issue is they aren't investing in one another to begin with and they constantly have arguments about living paycheck to paycheck. Their priorities are non-existent, yet they call each other partners.

Your partner in life should make sure you and your family is secure even after his/her life passes on. But it requires both of you to be on the same page. The trust will prove progression and responsibility toward a strong union. This shows that your investments need to be protected and appreciated. Study trust accounts and when it's important to implement them in your business and relationships. Do the research and determine if or which one is best for you. Get expert advice and speak with an attorney before making any decisions on opening a trust account.

Exercising Trust

What factors play into your ability or inability to trust the person you choose to be with?

What does your partner or potential partner need to do to earn your trust?

List some ways you and your partner can build trust in your relationship?

Here are some examples:

Say what you mean and mean what you say- A person can only respect you when you are honest and you follow through with what you say. Be clear and straight forward so there is no room for miscommunication.

Empathy- Have some empathy and try to understand where your partner is coming from with no judgement.

Be who you are- When both people can genuinely and unapologetically be themselves in a relationship it brings respect and loyalty to the forefront.

....

SECURITY

BLAC HEARTBEAT #5

1.   *the quality or state of being secure as it relates to danger, fear or anxiety*

2.   *something given, deposited, or pledge to make certain the fulfillment of an obligation*

"Security is Not a Product, But a Process"- Unknown

Some people think security is a "good job", 401k and benefits. If you get fired or get laid off, you lose the "security" don't you, then how is that security? Some people think security is relying on a partner that is well off financially to provide for their future. If their priority is their money and not the relationship, your security will always be in jeopardy. This is why it's best to create opportunities for financial freedom with your partner.

Financial security is the result you get when you follow the process of making sound decisions that lead you (and your partner) down the road to financial freedom. The decisions you make along the way are made with one underlining goal in mind, financial security and freedom. The type of financial security that allows you to not have to worry about your financial stability in the future. Not worry about your relationship, your finances or your wellbeing. Financial Security also gives you the freedom to explore your dreams and feel safe in your relationships. It gives you the time necessary to care for you and your family, to share moments with them and to have peace of mind in knowing they will be ok.

Emotional Security in Relationships

Emotional security in a relationship is just as important as financial security is. When you build trust, have respect, have consideration, exhibit integrity, dependability and responsibility you create emotional stability in your relationships. You don't leave your mate wondering how you will handle yourself when faced with a challenge or temptation. You offer your mate surety in a world filled with uncertainty. Emotional security in a relationship is the safe place within your relationship that you know, no matter what, your partner has your back and you have theirs. That you are willing to follow him/her to the ends of the earth and back because you know they will never mislead you under any circumstances.

It's during the period between becoming friends and courtship that you should be assessing the emotional state of the person you are considering for a relationship. Listen, Observe and Question are the 3 rules you should apply during this period.

1. Listen to EVERYTHING that person says.

2. Observe EVERYTHING that person does.

3. Ask Question about EVERYTHING

Not everybody you meet is emotionally stable. Sometimes it's not as prevalent in some people as in others, but if you Listen, Observe and Question, if there are any emotional issues you will see a few red flags.

You know what we're talking about. When you hear someone "Talkin' Crazy" take a minute and assess their mental stability, it might change the way you respond to that person. A lot of times people ignore the red flags and then find themselves in a very emotionally volatile relationship. Don't be that person who wants to play the savior role when you know someone has issues that will bring drama to your life just for the sake of saying you're with someone.

Communication is key to building emotional security. Many relationships fail due to lack of communication or miscommunication, which can lead to misconception about an issue that needs to be addressed. Without communication you may be looking at issues in a way that's far different then the way your partner is looking at it.

Here's a few warning signs to look for when assessing someone's emotional stability.

- Are they clingy?
- Need lots of attention?

- Need to be right ALL the time?
- Can't take constructive criticism?
- Has more low moments then high moments?
- Very pessimistic about everything?
- Offers more excuses than solutions?
- Plays the blame game?

There are many warning signs and red flags. Listen, Observe, Question. Feeling insecure can cause a person to become clingy or needy.

If you have openly and honestly embraced, discussed and accepted each message from The Five BLAC Heartbeats of Love and Wealth (individually or with a partner) you are (already) on your way to building emotional security in a future or current relationship.

Here's some other simple things you can do to enhance the emotional security within an existing or future relationship.

1.   Get in touch with your own emotions and emotional state.
2.   Let go of insecurity in relationships. Rather than always looking to the other person to

make you feel secure in your relationship, get into the habit of reassuring yourself.

3.   Be Present- Actively listen to your partner as they speak. Pay attention to body language and learn how they communicate.

4.   Breathing Space- Having to have your partner by your side at all times doesn't allow for the needed space to grow as individuals within your relationship.

Relationship and Family Business

It starts with partnership. As the saying goes, when two people agree on something, so it is! In the business world, a security is the contract of ownership. It's the deed to your car or home. It's the certificate of stocks and bonds that says you own this many shares at this price.

In marriage, it's the marriage certificate. The document that says this person is who I've invested my life with and now we are the "property" of each other. When you and your partner define security for you two, then you'll agree from the beginning that security and freedom is the ultimate goal and you will both take pride in working together to develop a plan to get there. Even if challenges arise during the process (which they will), as a team you will be so focused on the goal that getting through those challenges together will be light work.

If you both decided to invest in stocks for your children, then the children will have security certificates that show ownership of those stocks. Don't we want our kids to develop ownership skills early on? If your son loves to play basketball and loves to wear Nike sneakers, for birthdays or special occasion buy him a few shares of the stock. This way he can learn, if he's going to spend money with these companies, why not have some type of ownership in the company. This type of information and teaching build children's character and confidence early on and leads to more responsible wealth educated family and community members.

Side Note: Life Insurance- Get You Some! Don't leave your loved ones without a way to pay for expenses upon your passing. There are 2 guaranteed things in this world, birth and death. Make sure you are prepared for both.

Security Stocks

Keep this list to write down different companies that you would want to buy stock in. Or buy some for your kids, family or friends.

By using the space below write down the company, the price of 1 share and the date. Set a goal and in 90 days, purchase at least 1 share of stock. Keep going until the sheet is done and you have security certificates to show for each one.

● ●

Conclusion

We've all heard the tips, suggestions and unofficial rules of dating and maintaining a relationship but if it's not working drop it and focus on what you can do to invest in yourself and build with your partner. Most people's goal in life is to live free and be happy. Defining what happiness and wealth mean to you is the ultimate key. You are responsible for creating the vision of your life and relationships without any limitations or boundaries and the result of your vision will be heavily influenced by the person you choose to invest in.

It's a bold decision when you choose not to settle for less than you deserve. When you claim your confidence and self-worth you are making a commitment to yourself to only be with someone who will appreciate you and bring just as much value to your life.

We must not lose sight of why this book was written, we must not forget the importance of using the Five BLAC Heartbeats in business as it relates to our relationships. When you review the Five BLAC Heartbeats in relationships and compare it to certain aspects of business you will see the direct correlation that becomes a recipe for success. Why continue to date and be with people who are not helping you grow or get ahead? We have the most powerful source at our disposal and once we choose to use it in a way that can bring forth true happiness and wellbeing, we can rebuild families, create legacies and takeover our communities. Let's change the way we look at relationships and be conscious of the people we choose to impact (good or bad) our lives.

Start by asking yourself who am I, what do I want and what do I need? What do I bring to the table in a relationship? What is my vision for my life and where am I along that journey? Get a clear understanding of self, your wants, your needs, your strengths and weaknesses. Once you evaluate the areas you need to work on and take action you are on your way to love and wealth.

• •

Acknowledgements

We would like to give a special thanks to all who have supported BLAC Heartbeat from the beginning.

We would like to thank our mothers for building us up to be the strong individuals we are. And our fathers for showing us what it means to always go after what you want and never give up. We especially want to thank each other. We are best friends, partners and lovers. Without our union and our family, we would not have accomplished all that we have. We are soulmates that will cherish each day spent together on this earth.

What is Your Biggest Investment?

Your Mind Is Your Greatest Asset

True Love is Unconditional

Castle Cleanout LLC

Campbell Family Foundation

BLAC Love Still Exists

When Business Meets Pleasure

Play Together Get Paid Together

****

Booking and Contact

Queen Tiffany Geselle and King Donte

Married Mastermind Duo

Bestselling Authors

*

Business Owners

*

Relationship Strategists

"Build it. Love it. And. Commit to it. You'll be successful every time" – BLAC Heartbeat

Let's Build!

- **Speaking Engagements**
- **Seminars/ Conferences**
- **Interviews**
- **Youth Programs**
- **Network Partnership**

If you would like more information on

The Campbell Family Foundation Youth Entrepreneur Program please visit **www.TheCampbellFamilyFoundation.org**

BLAC Pathway to Success

Coming Soon!

Contact us for details!

BLACheartbeat@gmail.com

www.BLACheartbeat.com

Follow Us on

IG * FB * Youtube

@BLACheartbeat

Invest With

The

Person

You

Invest In

-BLACheartbeat